DEAR DAVE ~

WELL IT LOOKS LIKE I MAY HAVE BEEN A LITTLE OVERLY ENTUSIASTIC ABOUT YOUR CARTOONING POTENTIAL. IN FEAR OF LEADING YOU UP SOME DARK AND DANGEROUS ARTISTIC ALLEY, I THOUGHT I'D BETTER GET SOME PROFESSIONAL FEEDBACK. NOW, I WOULD NEVER PRESUME TO SEND A CARTOON OF YOURS (BUT IS ANYTHING REALLY ANYBODY'S?) TO A MAGAZINE WITHOUT YOUR PERMISSION SO I TOOK THE LIBERTY OF REDRAWING IT, THEREBY ENHANCING THE POSSIBILITY OF IT BEING ACCEPTED.* ALSO, I THOUGHT THAT MY NAME MIGHT GIVE IT SOME EXTRA ATTENTION OR CONSIDERATION, SO I TOOK THE ADDED TROUBLE OF SIGNING IT (DON'T THANK ME) WELL, DAVE, THE NEWS IS NOT GOOD.

THEY LOOKED AT THIS PIECE OF SHIT (THEIR WORDS NOT MINE) AND FAILED TO FIND ANYTHING HUMOROUS OR AMUSING IN IT. WELL, AT FIRST I ADOPTED A "FUCKEMWHATDOTHEYKNOW" ATTITUDE, BUT AFTER THE SIXTH REJECTION, I HAD TO FACE THE POSSIBILITY THAT THEY MAY BE RIGHT THAT EVEN WITH MY ~~DRAFTMANSHIP~~ DRAWING AND SIGNATURE YOUR CARTOON IS .. WELL .. NOT UP TO SNUFF.

IT TOOK NUMEROUS PHONE CALLS, VISITS, AND A FEW PRICEY LUNCHES FOR ME TO CONVINCE THEM THAT THIS WAS NOT MY CARTOON - BUT YOURS AND I WAS ONLY ACTING IN THE CAPACITY OF FRIEND AND ADVISOR: ONLY MY CREDIBILITY SAVED ME.

IN ANY CASE DAVE, YOU STEPPED UP TO THE PLATE AND YOU TOOK A FEW SWINGS. I SINCERELY BELIEVE THAT YOUR ~~THE~~ POSITION AS AMERICAS FOREMOST PLAY WRITE IS SECURE ENOUGH THAT YOU NOT NEED ~~TO~~ ADD "CARTOONIST" TO YOUR LEGEND - BUT NOT SECURE ENOUGH TO WEATHER AN ASSOCIATION WITH A FAILED ART FORM. THINK ABOUT IT

* HAD IT BEEN, WE COULD HAVE WORKED OUT SOME EQUITABLE SHARING OF ROYALTIES, BUT HEY, THAT'S ALL ~~ACADEMIC~~ IRRELEVANT

NO
GA

So I say count your blessings, your successes, your wonderful wife, your magical child, your many friends - and remember, Dave - plays - movies - books - essays - teaching - parenting - Talmudic studies - Dave, nobody is everything than ever will be consciously aware of Thurber, Steinberg, or myself. I mean that.

Love, Shel

I'm enclosing our Dear Wilde. Someday we may look back on this whole cockamamie attempt and even smile.

S.

JOHN WAYNE IN THE REPTILE HOUSE

THAT'S A BOA CONSTRICTOR.

Tested on Orphans—Cartoons by David Mamet, published by Trillium Press.

All cartoons copyright © 2006 David Mamet.

Letter from Shel Silverstein used by permission and copyright © 2006 the Estate of Shel Silverstein.

This publication marks the first in a series of comercially available books published by Trillium Press.

Book designed and imaged by Noah P. Lang.

ISBN 0-9727533-2-X

www.trilliumpress.com

PRINTED IN SINGAPORE

TESTED ON ORPHANS

CARTOONS BY
DAVID MAMET

WITH AN INTRODUCTORY
LETTER
BY SHEL SILVERSTEIN

DEATH VALLEY GIRL

NEWEST HIGH-CONCEPT RESTARAUNT

FROM: "SMALL BUSINESS STRATEGIES" ©
CREATE A SENSE OF URGENCY
FINE DRYCLEANING
SINCE 1951
FINE DRYCLEANING
UNTIL 2006
WRONG
CORRECT

"SUICIDE SLING"

OR

"THE INGEMAR BERGMAN"

INGREDIENTS:

A BUCKET OF VODKA.

A LEMMING.

51

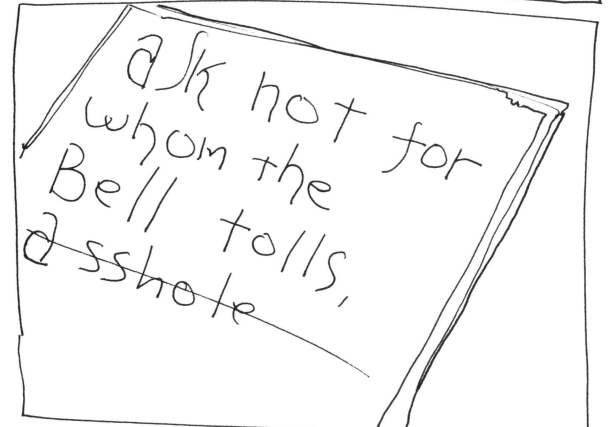

FAMOUS FIRST DRAFTS, CONT'D.
#5: TENNYSON

volley'd & thundered
stormed with shot and shell
Into the Jaws of Death
Into the mouth of Hell
... oh well...

EMERGENCY VETERINARY PROCEDURES

DIAGNOSING CANINE
MUNCHAUSEN SYNDROME

STEP ONE:

WOOF

TAKE THE HISTORY

ANNALS OF EXECUTIVE THOUGHT: THE SEQUEL

...AND THIS IS MY
SIGNIFICANT OTTER.

FROM THE DESK OF PAUL REVERE

TO DO:

BUY SILVER POLISH.

PLAN TEA PARTY.
   THEMES - ?
   ~~RUBBER~~
   ~~"ALL PINK"~~
   INDIANS
   ~~BEATNIK~~
   ~~SPACEMAN~~

—GRACE...? FOUR LETTERS: "HELLO," "WATCH OUT," OR "MAY I PLEASE HAVE SOME ATTENTION?" — "W" BLANK BLANK "F"...

HISTORIC FASHION VICTIMS #7:
1194 ~ THE FIRST KILT

...YOU'RE SURE...?

TRUST ME.

BUY ORGANIC!

UNHAPPY, CRUELLY
RAISED CHICKEN —

HAPPY,
ORGANIC
CHICKEN

RAISED WITH
BOTH FEET
NAILED TO THE
FLOOR

ONLY ONE
FOOT NAILED
TO FLOOR!

ROADSIDE ADVERTISING

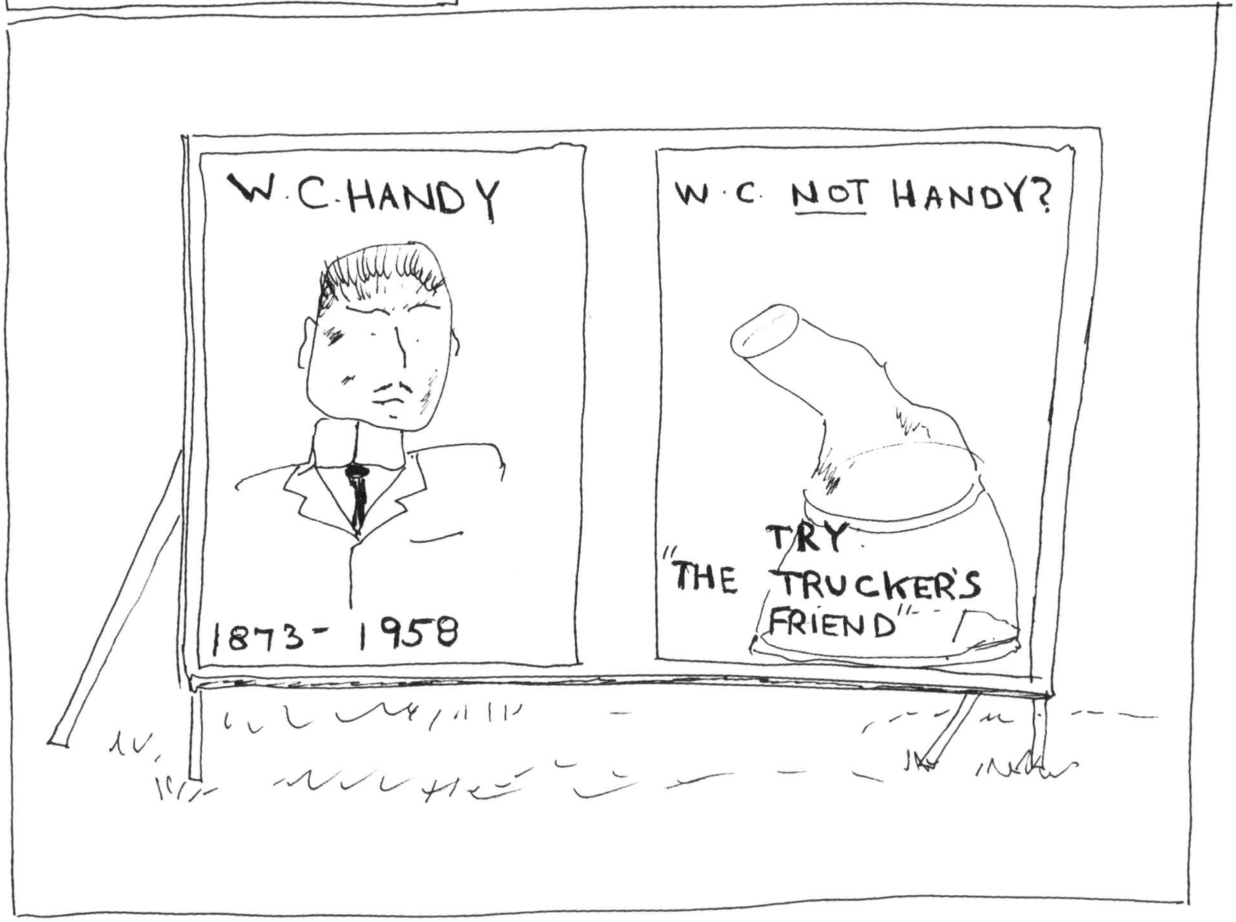

REAL-LIFE UNDERSEA DRAMA! THE ELECTRIC EEL REVEALS TO HIS PARENTS THAT HE'S A.C-D.C.

EVOLUTION OF A MASTERPIECE

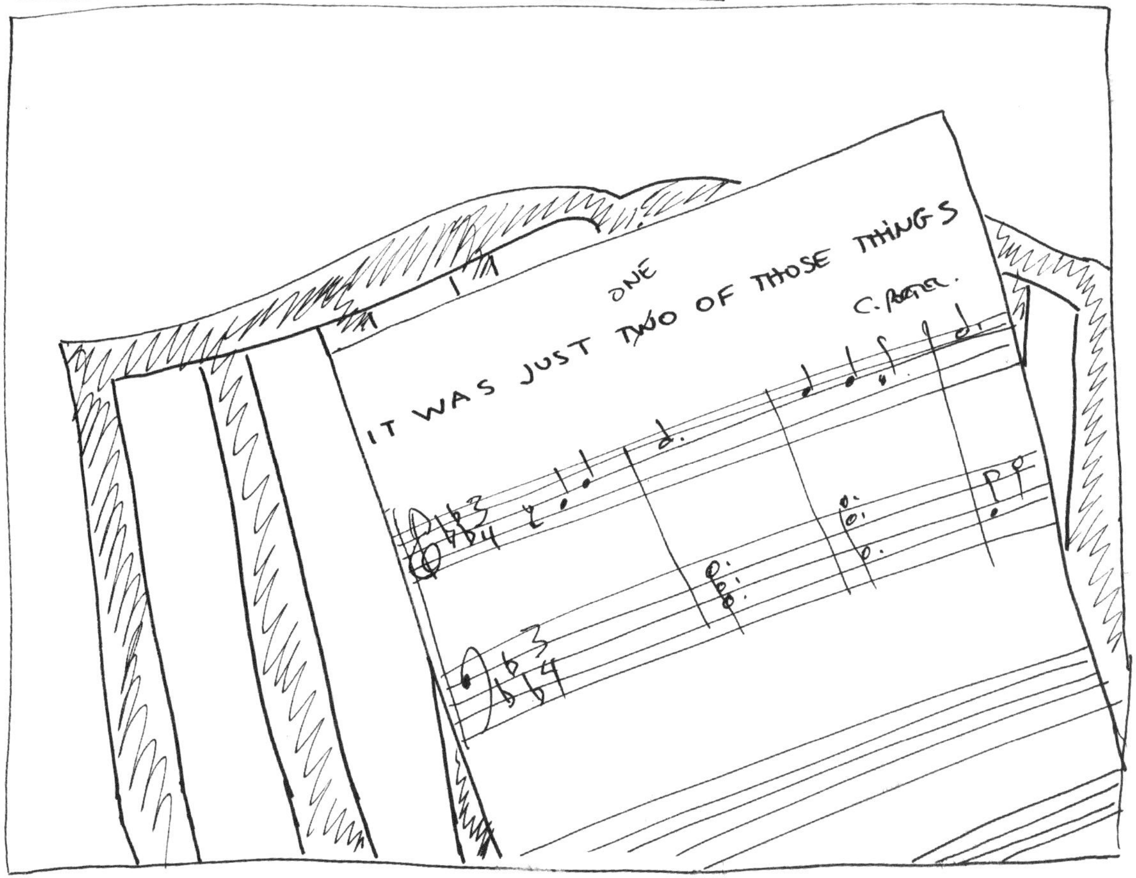

1959: FATS DOMINO AND CHUBBY CHECKER DOMINATE AMERICAN MUSIC—JAPAN RESPONDS:

CORPULENT G-O

JUSTIN,
THE CROSS-DRESSING
ZEBRA

WORLD'S WORST GREETING CARD

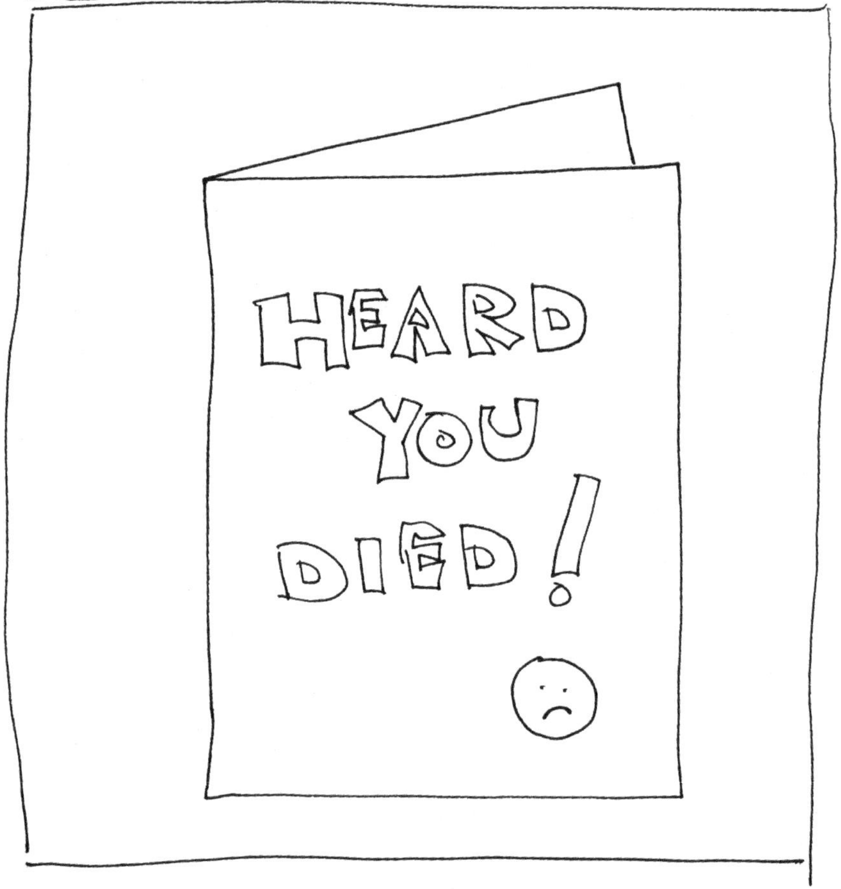

IF KANT HAD BEEN A VALLEY GIRL (c)

#5: "THE CRITIQUE OF PURE REASON"

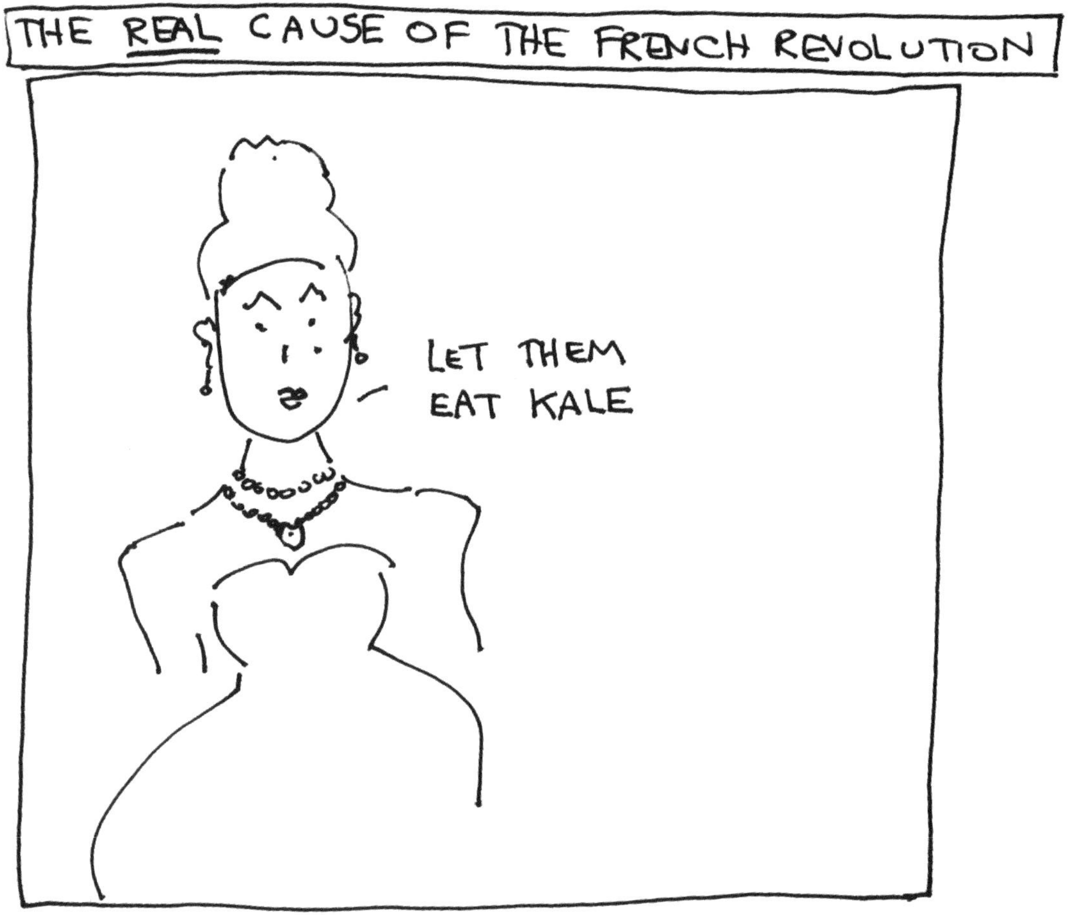
THE REAL CAUSE OF THE FRENCH REVOLUTION
LET THEM EAT KALE

OUR CRITIC PICKS:

STEVEN FOSTER, CABINETMAKER

THIS WEEK, THE AUTHOR OF "JEANNIE WITH THE LIGHT BROWN HAIR" LEARNS HOW TO MAKE A DOVETAIL MORTICE. (RERUN). 8:30 P.M. CH 432.

NOW, IT HAS BEEN POINTED OUT THAT IN 4 OF YOUR LAST 5 FILMS— YOU WERE SPAWNING...

IT WAS NECESSARY TO THE SCENE

MAKING THE SCHOLASTIC APTITUDE TEST ©
MORE ATTRACTIVE TO THE YOUNG [SAMPLE]

MARIE CURIE :

☐ A) HAD REAL BIG NIPPLES

☐ B) DISCOVERER OF RADIUM

☐ C) BOTH

☐ D) INSUFFICIENT INFORMATION

"METHOD CAT-CHARACTER ACTOR"
LESSON FOUR: EMOTIONAL MEMORY.

BEST   PICTURE

☐ _____

☐ _____

☐ _____

☐ _____

☐ _____

BEST   PERFORMANCE
BY AN ACTOR IN
A LEADING ROLE

☐ _____

☐ _____

☐ _____

☐ _____

☐ _____

WORKS AND PLAYS
WELL WITH OTHERS

☐ _____

☐ _____

☐ _____

☐ _____

☐ _____

SCHOOLROOM INJUSTICE · SWITZERLAND - 1896
HERR PROFESSOR: WHY IS IT - ? I BLOT MY COPYBOOK AND I AM PUNISHED - BUT WHEN ZIGGY RORSCHACH BLOTS HIS COPYBOOK, HE IS REWARDED ...?

PAROCHIALISM IN LITERATURE, CONT'D.
"... BY MIDNIGHT, OR ELSE THEY WOULD NOT BE CHANGED BACK INTO A PUMPKIN..."

ANNALS OF EXECUTIVE THOUGHT #3
CONCEPT SKETCH - DISNEY DEVELOPMENT TEAM CONSIDERS MAKING 'REMEMBRANCE OF THINGS PAST'!
"C'MON, FELLAS — SWANN'S IN TROUBLE...!"

SCHINDLER'S "B"-LIST

PAT O'BRIEN
RONALD REAGAN
MARIE WINDSOR
GEORGE TOBIAS
JAMES GLEASON

FAY WRAY
YAKIMA CANUTT
NATALIE KALMUS

BURMA SHAVE GOES TO NEW HAMPSHIRE

AND
TRAVE

AND, SORRY
I COULD NOT
TRAVEL BOTH

IN A YELLOW
WOOD

TWO ROADS
DIVERGED

SIGMUND FREUD EDITS HIS PAPERS FOR POSTERITY
ACK QUACK
K QUACK.
THE ROAD TO
ET TO THE
THER SIDE
HA HA HA.
EANS, BECAUSE
THEY MAKE ME
FART
RESISTANCE IS THE
NEUROSIS.
WOMEN LIKE
FELLAS WITH A
G DOOZER

DEAN MARTIN AT THE AQUARIUM

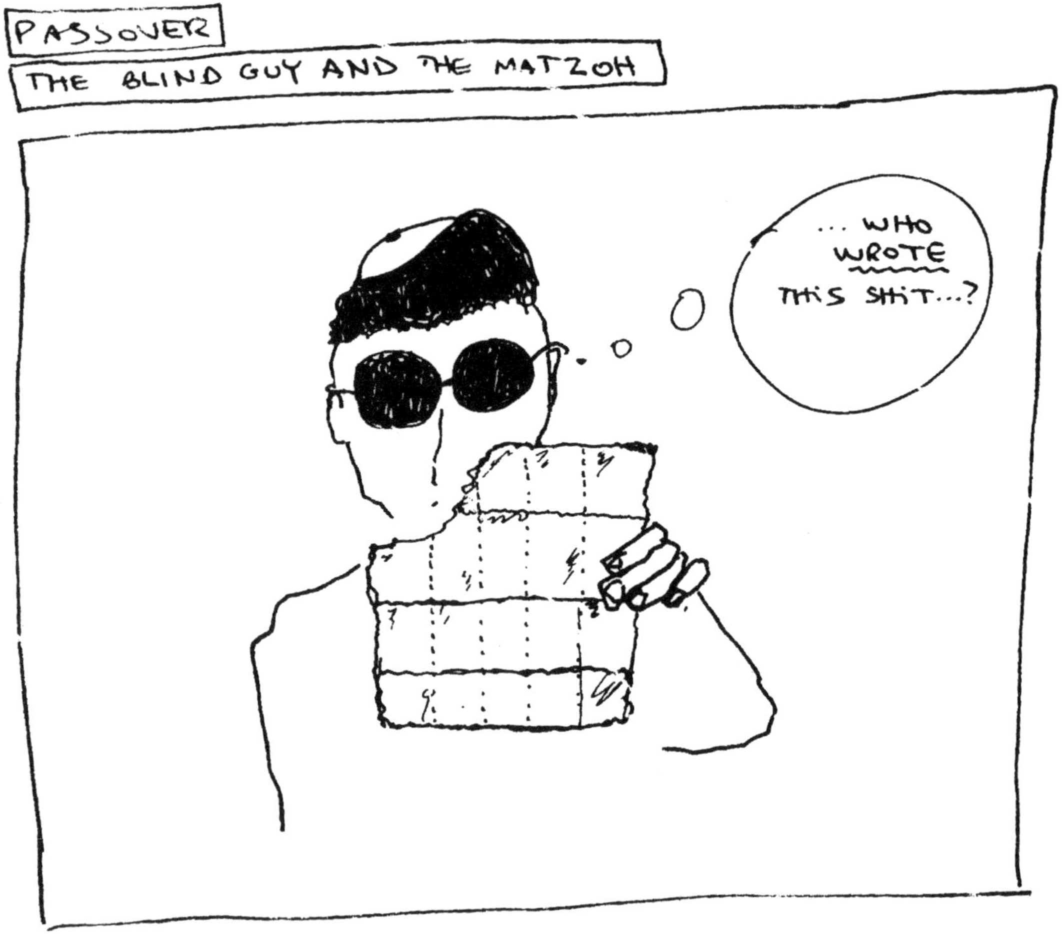
PASSOVER
THE BLIND GUY AND THE MATZOH
... WHO WROTE THIS SHIT...?

BOLD NEW START-UP

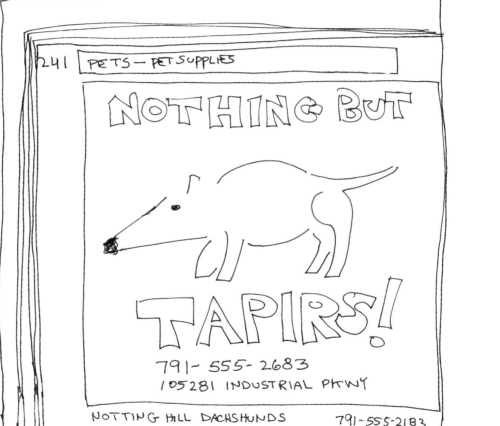

241 | PETS — PET SUPPLIES

NOTHING BUT
TAPIRS!
791- 555- 2683
105281 INDUSTRIAL PKWY

NOTTING HILL DACHSHUNDS   791- 555- 2183
NUT-BROWN BUDGERIGARS   791- 555- 0200

KNOW THE TERROR —
KNOW THE FEAR
RUMPEL-
STILTSKIN!
HE MADE
THEM GUESS
HIS
NAME!

LEARNING
TO TIE
YOUR
INNER SHOE

IDEAS AHEAD OF THEIR TIME:

THE FIRST HEART PACEMAKER: 1842

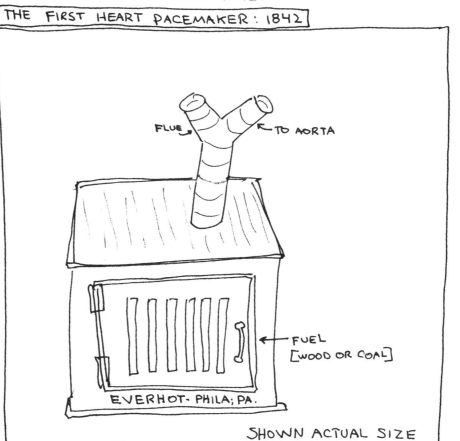

FLUE — TO AORTA

FUEL
[WOOD OR COAL]

EVERHOT-PHILA; PA.

SHOWN ACTUAL SIZE

U.S. FOREST SERVICE
PROTOTYPE POSTER AND COMMENTS
ONLY YOU CAN PREVENT FOREST FIRES
HATE THE SLOGAN
JANE
CAN WE CHOOSE A MORE BUTCH NAME? "BUZZ", OR "THAD"?
DOES IT HAVE TO BE A KANGAROO?

DIARY OF
HELEN OF TROY

FRIDAY MARCH XVI

Slow day.
Launched 3
ships.

THURSDAY NIGHT DYNAMITE!

8:00 E·ST.

"THANKS FOR NOTHING"

THE STORY OF A BOY RAISED BY ANTEATERS 5278412

9:00 E·S·T.

HOMAGE TO CATALONIA

THIS WEEK: CATALONIA STEPS IN TO SAVE THE DAY WHEN MRS. GRIMMIS BURNS THE STEW ·Ⓡ 6714218

ANNALS OF EXECUTIVE THOUGHT:
IDEA IDEA IDEA!
COMBINE POPULARITY OF J. AUSTEN NOVELS w/ A "RESORT DESTINATION" FOR OUR READERSHIP:
JAYNE MANSFIELD PARK
HUH !!!!!
DISCUSS.

HISTORIC ERRORS OF INDUCTIVE REASONING.
#5: THE CHRISTIAN COALITION OPPOSES POODLES

MISS
JULIE
BY EITHER
AUGUST STRINDBERG
OR
HENRIK IBSEN

INSPIRED BY THE BEAUTY OF THE LEBROYER "WATERBIRTH" METHOD, THE HOSPICE MOVEMENT SEARCHES FOR A SIMILAR EXPERIENCE TO ENHANCE THE <u>END</u> OF LIFE

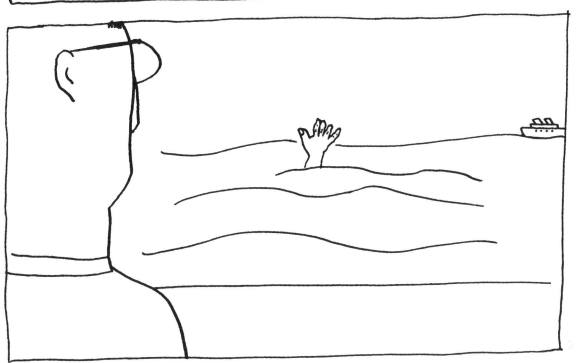

BUMPER STICKERS FOR OUR TIME #2

PRACTICE RANDOM ACTS OF
THOUGHTLESSNESS
AND INAPPROPRIATE EXPRESSIONS OF
CONTRITION

Hotel Bel-Arms

PLEASE INDICATE YOUR
PREFERENCE FOR READING
MATTER, AND IT WILL BE
PLACED OUTSIDE YOUR DOOR
IN THE MORNING.

☐ LOS ANGELES TIMES

☐ NEW YORK TIMES

☐ FAUST

LOS ANGELES, U.S.A.

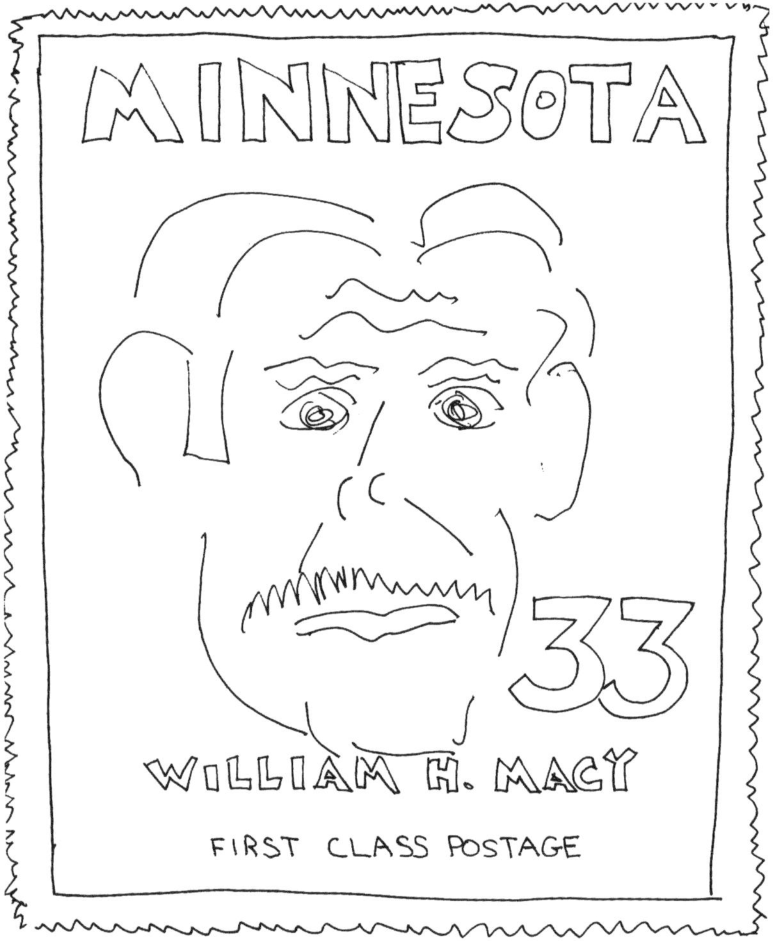
MINNESOTA
33
WILLIAM H. MACY
FIRST CLASS POSTAGE

THE TELEVISION PITCH IN COLONIAL AMERICA

106

THE TEMPEST

FULL FATHOM FIVE
THY FATHER LIES.
THOSE ARE SHELLS WHICH
WERE HIS EYES.
OF HIS BONES IS CORAL
MADE.
NOTHING IN HIM THAT
DOTH FADE
BUT DOTH SUFFER A
SEX CHANGE

D
P
DRA-
A-
IN
OW
RN
NAL:
RD

PAUL REVERE GOES HAT SHOPPING

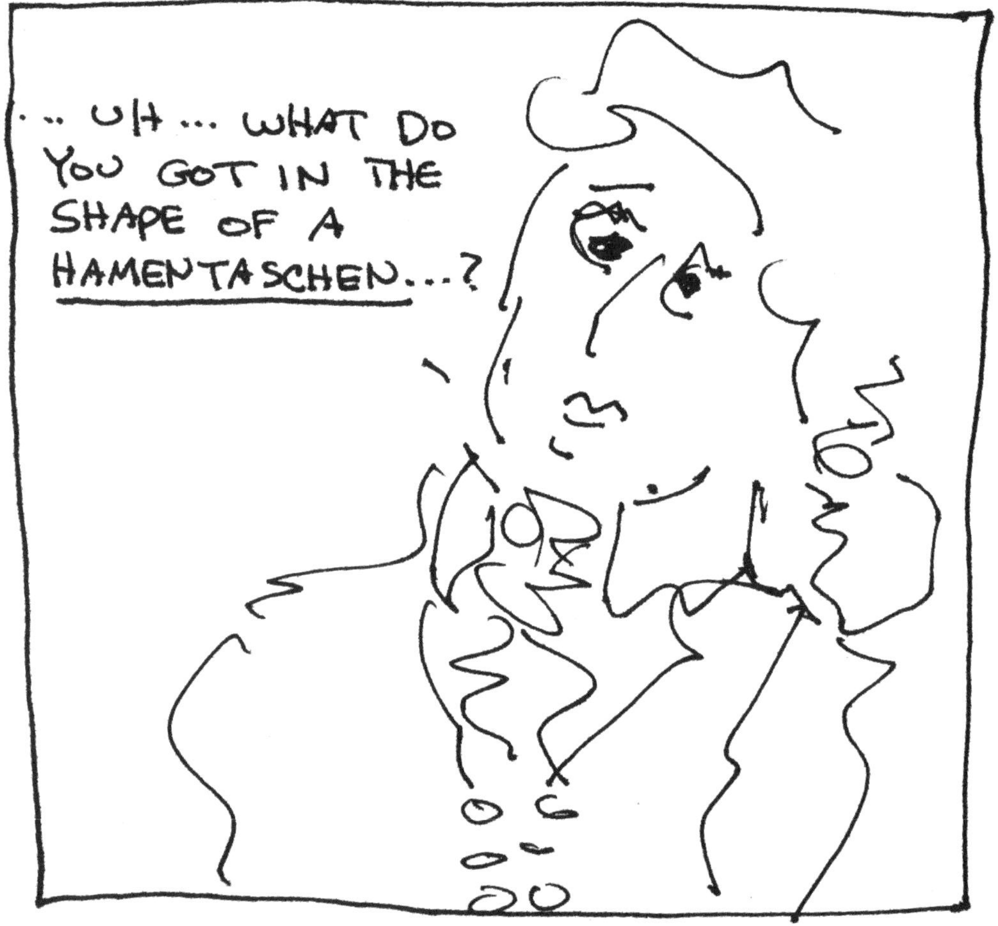

"SWEET LITTLE SCHIELE"
— GUSTAV KLIMT. —

ANNALS OF EXECUTIVE THOUGHT #2

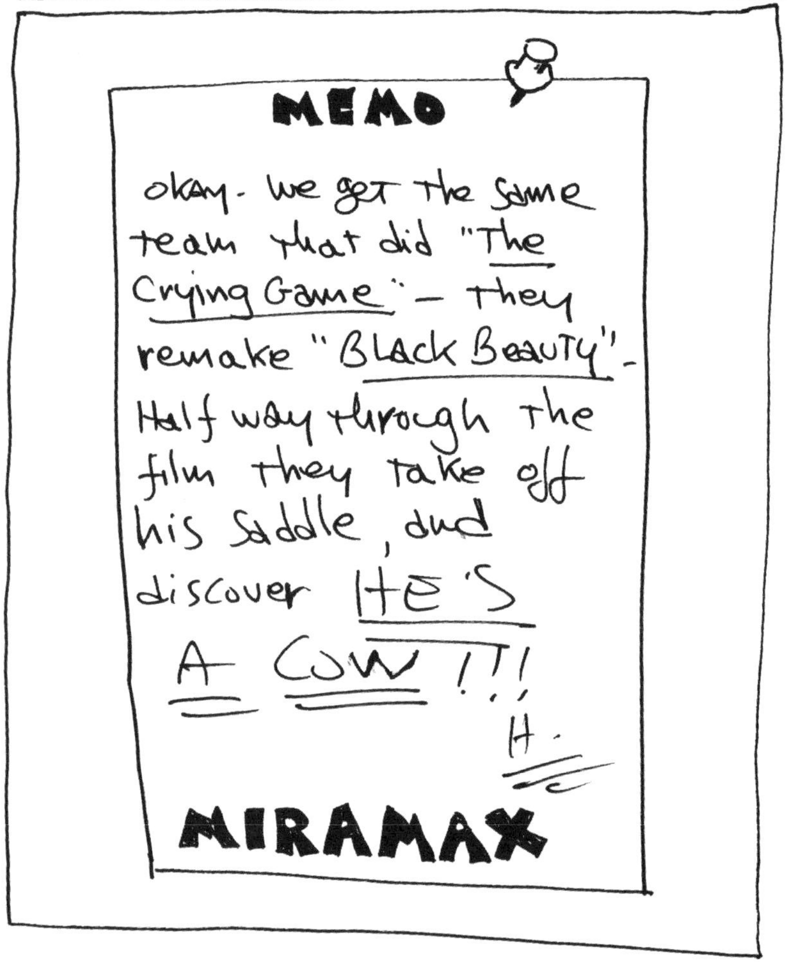

Deep and Barbara
Throat
Request the honor of
your company
at the marriage of their
Daughter,
Francesca,
To mister
Richardo